Crimes against Rhymez

CARL WEBBER

Copyright © 2020 Carl Webber

All rights reserved.

ISBN: 9798708072351

DEDICATION

This book is dedicated to all the front line workers and all the key workers that have risked their lives during the pandemic of 2020/2021. Especially my wife Louise and daughter Abi.

Thank you.

CONTENTS

Acknowledgements

1	The cat fell off	Pg 10
2	Crab apples	Pg 12
3	The mushrooms dance	Pg 14
4	Athletic veg	Pg 16
5	Catapulted	Pg 18
6	Ever nevers	Pg 20
7	River full of juice	Pg 22
8	Bumfuzzler	Pg 24
9	Grass	Pg 26
10	Legs of butter	Pg 28
11	Wondering chap	Pg 30
12	Drizzle and fizz	Pg 32
13	P&P	Pg 34
14	Riddles and rhyme	Pg 36
15	They stare	Pg 38

16	Lyrical limpet	Pg 40
17	Helen	Pg 42
18	The circus	Pg 44
19	The quack	Pg 46
20	Gamma rays	Pg 48
21	Prickly pears	Pg 50
22	Cornicook	Pg 52
23	Endless	Pg 54
24	A Kite	Pg 56
25	Pickle juice	Pg 58
26	The forest flea	Pg 60
27	Gingerbread jam	Pg 62
28	The Nastyling	Pg 64
29	Globby globs	Pg 66
30	The spoiled soup	Pg 68

ACKNOWLEDGEMENTS

Proof Read by Claire Bell
Cover Design by sidali_boudra on Fiverr
My Son Charlie for the inspiration for Wondering Chap "People!"

CRIMES AGAINST RHYMEZ

The cat fell off

Sorry, my cat fell off the cupboard and landed in your soup,
It splatted up the wall and covered the poor chicken, sleeping in his coup.

Sorry, my cat fell off the TV and landed on your lap,
It scared you so much that you screamed and your arms began to flap.

Sorry, my cat fell off the fridge and landed in the freezer,
He ate all your mums ice cream, that really didn't please her.

Sorry, my cat fell off the window sill and landed on your lamp,
It tipped over your glass of water and made the carpet damp.

Sorry, my cat fell off the table and landed on the chair,
He landed on all four feet, then sat just grooming his ginger hair.

Sorry, my cat fell off the bus and landed on the road,
He tumbled and rolled until he stopped, face to face with a rather large toad.

Sorry, my cat fell off the aircraft, his parachute no-where to be seen,
He didn't know if to laugh or cry, instead he decided to scream.

Sorry, my cat fell off the tree and landed in the pram,
The baby hit him with his teddy and made the cat scram.

Sorry, my cat fell off the moon and landed on the planet Mars,
There wasn't really much there, not even any chocolate bars.

I tied the cat to the chair,
Then he could not fall anywhere.

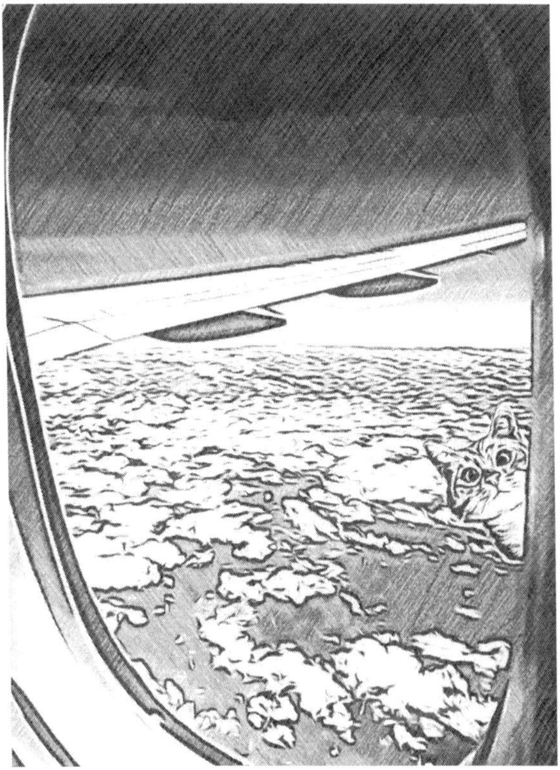

Crab apples

Crab apples lined the walkway,

to the house that wasn't a house,

Made of chocolate that wasn't chocolate,

nibbled by a duck billed platy mouse.

As you enter the front door, there is no bell to ring, if you wish,

just a rabid pot of tea

Fighting with a sugar dish.

Geppetto, was the master of the house,

His wife, her name was Sandy,

the lady of the house, who's face was made of cotton candy.

If you ever visit,

be prepared for what you see,

1 and 2 with 4 and 5 are sandwich made with 3.

CRIMES AGAINST RHYMEZ

CRAB APPLES... THEY LINED THE WAY

CRIMES AGAINST RHYMEZ

The mushrooms dance

When they go on holiday to France,

The mushrooms begin to dance.

They go swimming in the sea,

When they visit Italy.

They hike along the roads,

When they fly away to Rhodes.

They hook up the old caravan,

On their way to the Isle of Man.

They like to eat all the pizza,

When they go clubbing in Ibiza.

On their phones they like to talk,

Walking around the streets of New York.

They run as fast as they can,

when they go gardening in Iran.

When they finally return home,

They stand still in a field, like a garden gnome.

Athletic veg

The finish line seemed just out of reach,

for the legs pounding on the amazing running peach.

He was one of a kind, never before seen,

Like his vegetable cousin, the famous runner bean.

Almost as amazing is the high jumping apple,

built round and plump but amazingly supple.

The long jumping banana is a sight to be-hold,

but once got it wrong and he split I was told.

An onion that can throw the javelin so far,

better than being pickled and served in a jar.

But my favourite must be the hurdle jumping cucumber,

Always great to watch and always one to remember.

CRIMES AGAINST RHYMEZ

Is it a bird?
Is it a plane?
Is it a bear?
I think I'm going
insane!

CRIMES AGAINST RHYMEZ

Catapulted

Sat on the edge of his wooden, stolen chair,

Dark leathery skin and long grey greasy hair.

Was a guy who had one eye of glass,

Not worked a day in his life and just sat on his bone idol ass.

Fingers all crooked and teeth that matched too,

Two parrots for pets, one has the sneezing bird flu.

He snarls and spits, at all that walk by,

One poor lad copped a great greenie, right in the eye.

Until one day, this fowl nasty man met his match,

A pretty little girl but with a bad temper to dispatch.

She wondered over,

without a care in the world,

CRIMES AGAINST RHYMEZ

Her language was dark,

the old man had unfurled.

She tied a rope around the nasty man's legs,

What happened next caused quite a flare.

The rope was tied to a car and off it sped,

He was catapulted up into the air.

Screaming as he flew, over the houses,

He came to rest at the foot of an old oak tree,

A little girl had taught him a lesson,

Never again did that horrible man choose to be a bully.

CRIMES AGAINST RHYMEZ

Ever nevers

There is a place that is full of Trevors

Weird looking fellas all covered in feathers.

A strange looking land with chocolate covered books

Sheep with Reebok trainers, getting funny looks.

Fields full of dizzy wasps,

buzzing as they walk,

Banana flavoured goats who surprisingly like to talk.

Coffee filled catfish swim in the river,

Joke telling snakes,

all a quiver.

Flowers grey and wilting with shame,

Clouds of rusty nails, make rain a pain.

If you get to visit the Ever nevers,

Make sure you say hello to all the feather covered Trevors.

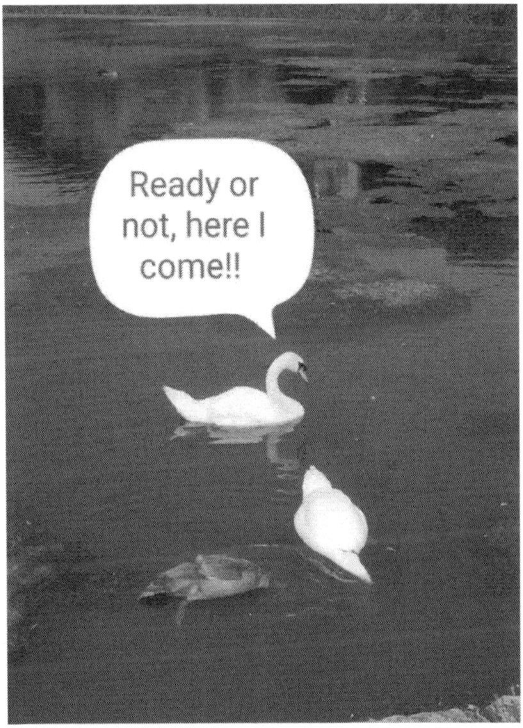
Ready or not, here I come!!

River full of juice

One dark night,

I dreamt of a river full of juice,

in it swam fish that you could catch,

with a rope tied like a noose.

They jumped like kangaroos,

bouncing through the outback bush,

Their little faces were smiling,

with a little hot flush.

They had arms which they used to wave,

A wave of 'Hello' not one to save!

Funniest looking fish that you wouldn't want to eat,

Not the kind of fish you would take home for your mother to meet.

CRIMES AGAINST RHYMEZ

I awoke from the dream,

covered in a splash of colour,

I had turned prickly pear orange,

Like the fish, oh what a bother.

Bumfuzzler

In a strange land, made of jelly and sand

a land that quite frankly was like sour milk, ever so boring and ever so bland.

There lived a creature no bigger than an imp,

you would be out of your mind to call him a wimp.

Strong as an ox and made out of lead,

eyes red like blood, quite scary it has to be said.

He would put you in situations of confusion and befuddlement,

your eyes glazing over with a look quite redundant.

Your mind just cannot understand,

all this turbulence leaving you face down in the sand.

His evil demeanour and bewildering stature,

creating overwhelming environments, your soul he will capture.

So if you ever come across him, Bumfuzzler his name,

don't look him in the eyes, he will drive you insane!

Grass

Crystals sat atop, adorning each glossy blade of grass,

I happily stepped upon them and fell straight on to my ass.

As pretty as it looked, it caused me so much pain,

I will never walk upon, that crystal topped grass again.

I came across some grass, this time it was topped with jelly,

I stepped upon it and fell forward right onto my belly.

As pretty as it looked, it caused me so much pain,

I will never walk upon, that jelly topped grass again.

I came across some grass, it was topped with bread,

I stepped upon it, fell backwards and banged my poor head.

As pretty as it looked, it caused me so much pain,

I will never walk upon that, bread topped grass again.

I came across some grass, it was topped with cheddar cheese,

I stepped upon it, I fell, and grazed both my knees.

As pretty as it looked, it caused me so much pain,

I will never walk upon, that cheese topped grass again.

I came across some grass, but decided to keep to the path.

Legs of butter

Stricken with a curse, her legs were made of butter,

Given by a witch doctor, by George he was a nutter.

This beautiful young gal, she was a damsel in distress,

She tried to cover her embarrassing butter legs, with a long flowing flowery dress.

Until one hot summer day, her legs started to melt,

Words could not explain how scared this poor gal felt.

She took to social media in search of some new legs,

Various options came, how about those wooden clothes pegs?

Then came a dairy expert, he made her melted legs a-new,

Now the damsel, able to walk, wasn't feeling so down and blue.

So she marched on with confidence, with the smell of victory in the air,

Her legs made of butter by the witch doctor nutter,

but now she really did not care.

Wandering chap

He's walking

he's talking

but he's not making any sense

stood talking and yapping

to next doors garden fence!

With his blanket in his hand

he's fresh out of bed

living out his dreams,

he's still asleep, have I said??

CRIMES AGAINST RHYMEZ

This is a plane!

Drizzle and fizz

Joel had an idea and his idea was quite mad,

He decided to start a business, one, that no one before had ever had.

His thought process rumbled as it tumbled from his brain,

Streaming from his mouth like a powerful locomotive steam train.

He told the world of his pioneering task,

Bubbling with excitement, but would it really last?

He set the wheels in motion and his dream started to come true,

Millions of pounds to be made and this he defiantly knew.

The time had come and he was ready to reveal his genius business,

something the world in anticipation didn't want to miss.

See Joel had created his dream and his dream was this,

A company selling free bottles of drizzle and of fizz.

Drizzle and fizz?? I hear you say,

How is this different? In what possible way?

Well the drizzle and fizz was joy and happiness in bottles you see

to distribute through out this world and spread a little glee.

How did he make his millions? By selling something that was free

Giving out joy and happiness is priceless, try it one day and you will truly see!!

P&P

Paupers and peppercorns,

Positively pass posing Peter.

Parading parrots pick pickled porpoises,

puckered pickers post pumpkin pie, paying postage & packaging

Potential penalty poses pain,

Probably parked perpendicular.

Place pen pointlessly positioned,

Paper portrays...

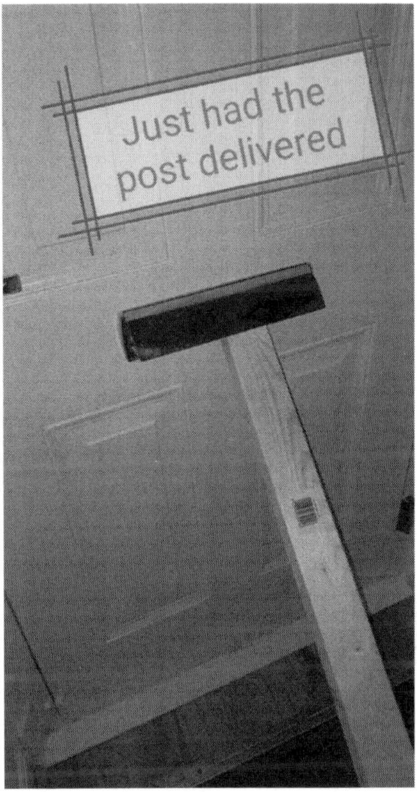
Just had the
post delivered

Riddles and rhyme

In the land of riddles and rhyme,

there is no distinction between reality and time.

Nothing makes sense and is all higgledy-piggle,

Playing hopscotch on turtles and piggy in the middle.

In this world, everything is all about face,

White is black and space is filled with something in its place.

Children are adults and adults are kids,

Cups are served upside down but without any lids.

Are you confused? Well I am too,

there is only one thing you can do,

Visit the land of riddles and rhyme,

perhaps on a train, choo choo.

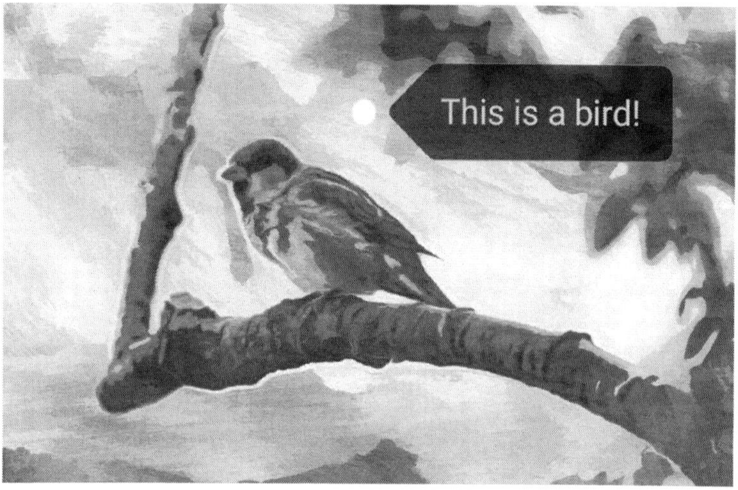
This is a bird!

CRIMES AGAINST RHYMEZ

They stare

You know the way that people stare,

Like you have a bogey hanging from your hair.

The glare that could burn a hole in your head,

Like you have served them dog poo in toasted bread.

You give them a wave but it doesn't deter,

am I an animal or a monster covered in fur?

It's really quite rude if you think about it too much,

Give them a picture, a selfie or such.

Why not just give them a real reason to stare so much,

Scream and shout, then hit them with your crutch!!

An old picture of my mum, isn't she lovely.

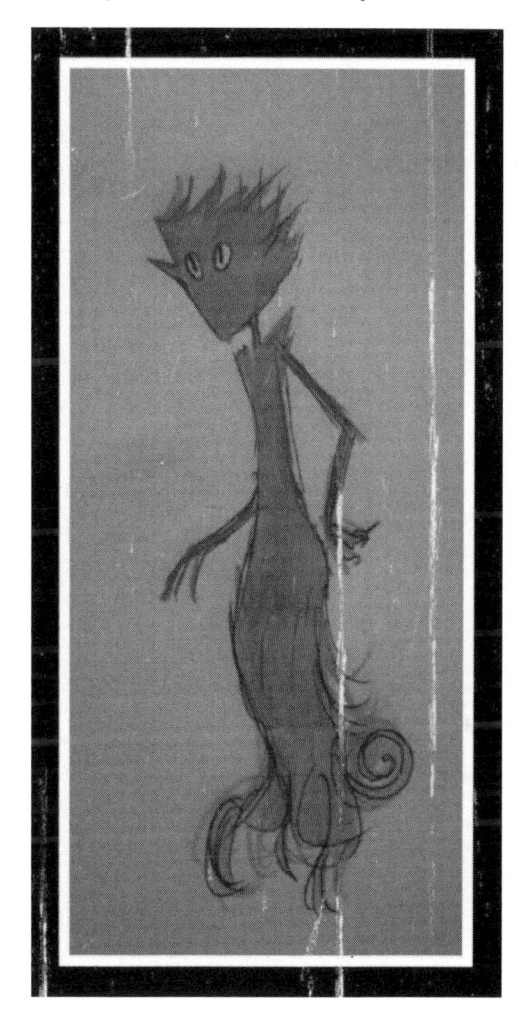

CRIMES AGAINST RHYMEZ

Lyrical limpet

Under water bubbles escape from his shell,

pockets of air rising up, give off a real bad smell.

But if you listen, with your ear stuck to the rock,

what you will witness, will come as quite a shock.

For these bubbles contain poetry, of the magical, lyrical kind,

some of the most beautiful story telling, you will ever find.

Poems filled with love, hope and of wisdom,

not just a sea dwelling shell as you have become accustom.

Next time you're at the seaside and you spot our poetic friend,

take time to have a listen, as to you, a poem he may send.

CRIMES AGAINST RHYMEZ

Helen

Helen was the local hairdresser,

a very popular one at that.

Until one day she got closed down for health and safety reasons,

now let me get this exact.

She had been trading as a kebab shop at night,

lucky for her she got away with a £180 fine.

You could say that was a close shave,

but it had been only a matter of time.

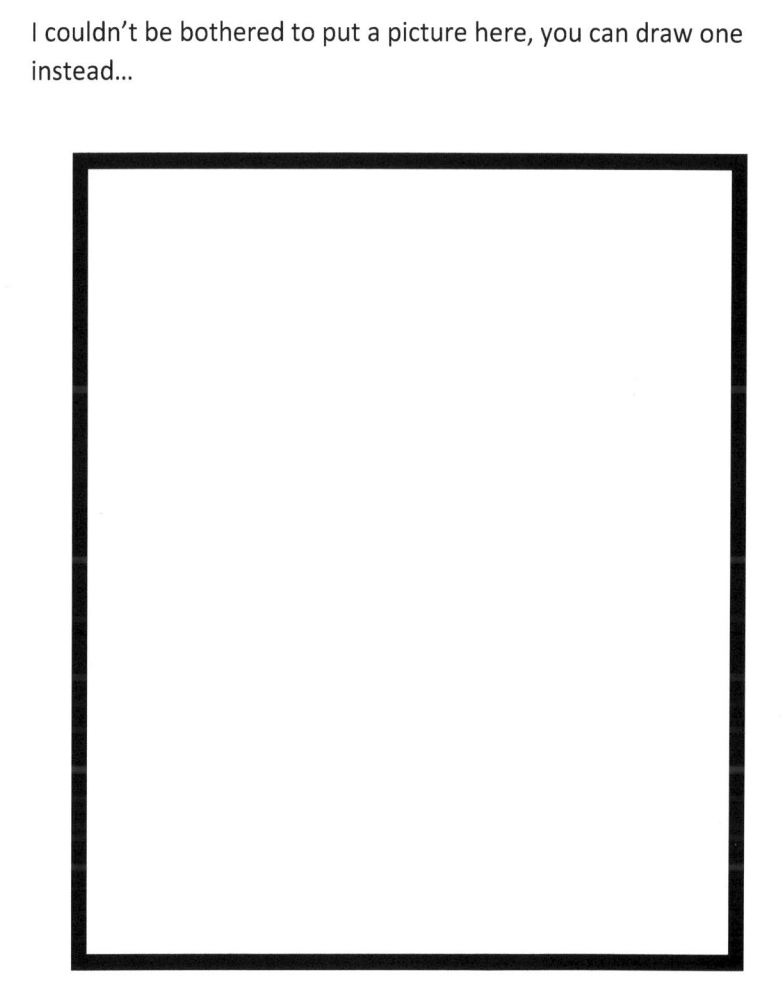

I couldn't be bothered to put a picture here, you can draw one instead...

The circus

The circus parade stumbled into town,

First came the big ring master, followed closely by the clown.

They set up their big top, in the middle of the field,

quite an erection I would say,

Putting posters all over town,

it took them most of the day.

People would come from miles around,

to see the entertainment that night,

Trapeze artists flying about and the strong man with all his might.

Laughter erupts from the clown in his car, as the wheels and doors fall off,

Water squirting flowers wet the front row, blowing his nose in someone's jacket they had taken off.

CRIMES AGAINST RHYMEZ

The lions are now banned and the elephants too, it was seen as much to cruel,

So instead two knife throwers square up in a death defying duel.

Even so at the end of the night, the audience go away happy,

Back next year the circus returns, without the chimpanzee in a nappy.

The quack

The quack came from the duck and was originally a sound,
until one day it came out as an object, really quite profound.

It was square and yellow with short little legs,
Coins for eyes, and arms that were pegs.

It waddled around quite a happy little thing,
It never spoke but used to dance and loved to sing.

If you ever encountered a quack you would surely know,
They made people happy wherever they go.

They live in chocolate rivers and liquorice trees,
Not in pepper bushes though because they make them sneeze.

You will never see a picture of a quack, they always run and hide,
Behind the nearest tree, or a house to go inside.

If you ever encounter a quack,

please do say Hello,

They will make your day so much better,

or even your week glow.

CRIMES AGAINST RHYMEZ

Gamma rays

Just the girl next door, mistaken as a lifeless nerd,

This girl was ready, she was just waiting to be heard.

Polite and cute, with beautiful long dark hair,

the darkest of eyes into which you could forever stare.

Today was the day, that changed her life forever,

The pieces of excitement were knitting perfectly together.

Set on a plan, to which she had no clue,

supernaturally guided, carefully shown what to do.

Taken to a barn, in which stood a mantle,

Glowing with a warmth, drawn in, must handle.

She softly touched the mysterious item,

Not a care for her well-being, to others it might frighten.

As her soft hands enveloped the light,

She was gripped by a force, an awe in plain sight.

Gamma rays, entered her veins, her brain was now reprogrammed,

A superhero made to protect, the world and most important, her home land.

This was a moment of which she had always dreamed,

now it had come true,

This once quiet girl transformed and now a hero,

No more hassle, no more questions of Who?

CRIMES AGAINST RHYMEZ

Prickly pears

Prickly pears were found on the rug,

Found by the purple, barefooted rhino drinking coffee from a mug.

Slippery tomatoes appeared on a bed,

Splattered all over the wall, when the pink lady went to sleep it was said.

Fun filled crepes flew aimless through the sky,

An old gentleman looked up and caught one straight in the eye.

2 Ducks and 4 flamingos posed for pictures in the park,

I went back that night, they were still there, even though it was dark.

Hungry clown fish searched for a bite to eat,

Chomping on newspaper or people that they meet.

Come to this place where it's strange and surreal,

after an hour here you start to think it is real.

Cornicook

I bet you have met one of these strange creatures before,

perhaps you never noticed, perhaps you never saw.

I'm telling you now with pinkie promises made,

they are joke telling folk, whose enthusiasm never fades.

They are not those kinda jokes that make your belly wobble and laugh,

or chuckle until you cry or until you wanna barf!

These jokes are so terrible they only laugh at them themselves,

usually got a million bad joke books,

piled up upon shelves.

They can come in many disguises, but they have a couple that they prefer,

like dads, uncles and granddads they are all quite the connoisseur?

So next time you hear a bad joke, make sure you take a close look,

as it could be a comical creature called a Cornicook.

A CORNICOOK AIN'T THAT FUNNY!!

Endless

Everlasting peppermint sticks with endless licks.

Cola drinks with endless sips.

Piranha bites with endless nips.

Bear arms with endless hugs.

UK weather with endless rain.

Oil tycoons with endless money.

Monks with endless faith.

Kentucky with endless chicken.

Children with endless love.

Work with endless days.

Grandmas with endless kisses.

Motorways with endless queues.

The list is Endless....

A Kite

Fairies and goblins frolic in this far away land,

Bubbles and sparkles, pretty twinkling sound.

Carefree and giggles abound this rainbow filled place,

Not one little creature without a smile on its face.

Clouds made of pillows that you could rest on and float away,

Sparkling clear water lapping up on a golden bay.

Birds trailing colour as they fly through the sky,

Not knowing where they are going, not caring why.

A kite sailed away, to catch itself a dream,

maybe the best hot chocolate filled with marshmallows and cream.

So come visit and see this beautiful place one day,

it is only one, one daydream away.

Pickle juice

Pickle juice, go on take a sip,

put a drop right there on your lip.

I just want to see your screwed up face,

Pickle juice, such a sour taste.

Your eyes start to water and mouth starts to wet,

Can I offer you a pint of pickle juice yet?

Hand slaps the table because you can't withstand,

the pickle juice is mighty, like illegal contraband.

Finally you give up the fight with the sour drink,

not a great tasting tipple, quite the opposite, don't you think.

CRIMES AGAINST RHYMEZ

The forest flea

How tired am I?

I'm as tired as can be,

not like the energy filled,

Little forest flea.

Day and night he bounces,

Sometimes he even flies,

when all I want to do is slowly shut my eyes.

Keeps a beady eye out for his next fur covered bus,

Hitch-hiking traveller no care, no fuss.

HOP,

    SPRING,

        BOING, he is off on a spurt,

Makes me tired just thinking about it, oh my eyes, they hurt.

If I could choose, what creature I could be,

I think I would definitely choose, to be the energetic flea.

Not a tired slimy slug, who can't be bothered to move his bones,

Yep, a slug, that's me you know, like a snail but without the home.....

Gingerbread jam

Pillowy petals floated down from the king size trees,

Dimwitted and dense was the fluffy bouncy forest in which they did what they please.

A remembered memory of a forgotten time,

When they were just young saplings of single proportion, ready for their prime.

Sulky but sweet was the side tables that they meet,

Gingerbread jam with mouthwatering ham covered their toppings where alarm clocks stand on their bell feet.

Moaning myrtle the English turtle would visit now and again,

Moaning about the filtered fluorescence shining through the pillowy petals, when...

Whitened and whittled the lamp of bedside shone,

Emulating billowy bubbles of bliss, sleep approaching, soon gone.

Transparent reactions, as sleep shows your true emotions,

Caught in the fluffy bouncy bed forest, nothing but sheep counting commotions.

The Nastyling

He has black curly hair all covered in grime,

a mad crazy stare, constantly stepping out of line.

Lives in a bunker, all covered in moss,

thinks he's the best and always the boss.

Lolloping around in his big clumpy boots,

stamping on helpless bugs and ripping up flowers by their roots.

He has not a care for the things of this world,

his pure nastiness and wrath continually unfurled.

The Nastyling is its name and if you ever did meet,

be sure if you're on a bus to offer him your seat.

CRIMES AGAINST RHYMEZ

This is what you can call an old person with greying hair...

Gobbly glops

Gobbly glops of gloop oozed into her soup,

From her nose the green slime fell,

what a nincompoop.

Nothing she did could stop the rapid flow,

No raccoon stuffed nostrils or into a tissue she tried to blow.

Still it poured out, like a storm cloud filled with buckets of rain,

her head tilted back and the loudest sneeze, out it came.

The gloop was now projectile and flying out like a jet-propelled plane,

I'm really quite surprised she didn't blow out some of her brain.

Then all of a sudden, the flow did stop,

Green gobbly glops of gloop still all over her top.

A cold she had, as she had gone to bed with her hair wet,

Constant dripping nose started glooping again, quick call the vet.

CRIMES AGAINST RHYMEZ

The spoiled soup

Scrapings from the bottom of the chicken coop,

Catfish fins and dogs eyebrows in my soup.

Add some toe nails and a pinch of sand,

the best tasting soup in all of the land.

Sweat from a bat, tears from a snail,

trump of a hybrid lama and a bunny's cotton tail.

Two more ingredients to finish this fine concoction,

Shrimps elbows and some baby lotion.

Two hours of simmering, some cornflour to thicken,

the spoiled soup had turned to gloop, like someone had been sick in.

> Anyone else stare at dead bodies in movies, to see if you can catch them breathing...

A big thank you for reading my book.

I hope you enjoyed my random rhymes and additional random pictures.

Keep an eye out for more books coming soon.

Carl

Get in contact with me at:

Email: carlwebber_@outlook.com

Social media accounts:

Instagram: carlwebber16

Twitter: @carlwebber16

Printed in Great Britain
by Amazon